Printed in China

Published by Justice and Spirituality Publishing
P.O. Box 5189
New Britain, PA 18901
U.S.A.

Web site: www.JSP.us

ISBN: 978-1-942482-00-0

Library of Congress Catalog Card Number: 2018950977

Printed on acid-free paper

Presented to:
Br. Najm

Presented by:
Br. Khalid

Date:
3-25-19

Keep us in your
Duaa,

“Truly, those who succeed are those who purify it [the soul]”

(Quran 91:9)

Contents

For Each Time There Is an Assigned Work

In the name of God, the Most Gracious, the Most Merciful: may His blessings and peace be upon His Prophet Muḥammad and the Prophet's *Āl al-Bayt*[1], Companions, Brethren[2], and Party[3].

Dear Brothers and Sisters in Faith:

The Lord - exalted is He - has proclaimed in Sūrat al-Mulk (67:2):

> *It is He Who has created Death and Life, that He may test which of you are best in deed.*

---

[1] Translator's note: The Prophet's family (*Āl al-Bayt*) comprises his wives; his grandsons al-Ḥasan and al-Ḥusayn; his uncle al-ʿAbbās; his paternal cousins ʿAlī, Jaʿfar, and ʿAqīl; and the descendants of all the aforementioned.

[2] TN: The Prophet's Brethren are the prophets and messengers who were sent before him, their believing wives, and their followers, men and women. They also include those men and women who have believed in the Seal of the Prophets without having met him, that is, the members of his community who have embraced Islam since his passing.

[3] TN: All Muslim men and women who serve Islam's cause and strive to unite the Muslim community worldwide.

Since your lifetime is your capital, it is imperative to learn how to manage each of life's tasks in turn. The point of life is not to do whatever you want, whenever you want; rather, the point is to learn how to do the right work at the right time. Therefore, you should learn the acts of the heart that are required for their prescribed time, the acts of the tongue for their prescribed time, and the acts of all your other organs at their prescribed times. When Abū Bakr aṣ-Ṣiddīq was nominating ʿUmar b. al-Khaṭṭāb as his successor, he counseled:

> *Know that the Lord has commanded us to perform certain acts in the daytime, which He will not accept for us to perform at night; and so too has He commanded us to perform certain acts in the nighttime which He will not accept for us to perform in the day.*

So how can you carry out all your obligations in such a limited lifespan so as to attain the bliss of this life and the Hereafter? In Sūrat an-Naḥl (16:97), the Lord (magnified be He) explains:

> *To those who work deeds of righteousness, men or women, and have faith, We will give a life that is good and pure, and We will bestow on them their reward according to the best of their actions.*

It is thus by faith and righteous deeds that felicity may be attained. As for faith, the Messenger (God bless him and grant him peace) has taught us that it is made up of seventy branches. Among these branches of faith[4] are certain acts

---

[4] TN: The branches of faith (*shuʿab al-īmān*) are those acts of worship (physical, moral, intellectual, and spiritual) that enable our journey toward spiritual excellence (*iḥsān*). Many scholars of *ḥadīth*, such as al-Bayhaqī and al-Ḥulaymī, have enumerated these branches as being sixty or seventy in number. In his *Prophetic Method* (al-Minhāj an-Nabawī), Imām Abdessalam Yassine has arranged them into the ten virtues (*al-khiṣāl al-ʿashr*) for training the believers to ascend the three stages of the faith (*islām, īmān, iḥsān*), this training being a sine qua non for the task of uniting Muslims worldwide.

that the believer[5] must perform at least once in their lifetime (such as the Pilgrimage); acts that are mandatory once a year (the Ramadan fast); acts that are prescribed at regular intervals (the ritual prayer [*aṣ-ṣalāh*] and ritual charity [*az-zakāt*]); acts that are mandated under particular circumstances (visiting the sick, paying last honors to the deceased, clearing away a public pathway that has been obstructed); acts that relate to individual virtues (modesty); and finally, acts that should be made into firmly-established habits (chanting the testimony of faith that "there is no god but God" [*lā ilāha illallāh*]).

The believer should cultivate habits that allow them to spend their time in worship and *jihād*[6] rather than frivolous worldly pursuits. As a gnostic[7] once taught:

---

[5] TN: By "believer" is meant not the ordinary Muslim who merely practices the five pillars of Islam, but is one who seeks to embody the branches of faith and thence aspires to *iḥsān*, spiritual excellence.

[6] TN: Often mistranslated as "holy war," *jihād* refers to the effort that the Muslim, man or woman, exerts to serve God as an individual or as a member of the community in all spheres of life.

[7] TN: A gnostic - literally, a "knower of God" (*ʿārif billāh*) - is a Sufi master or spiritual scholar who is firmly grounded in the quintessence of Islamic Law (*al-Ḥaqīqa*). In chapter 25, verse 59 of the Qurʾān, God (exalted be He) says: "God, the Most Gracious - ask those expertly informed of Him."

If anyone fails, for a single day of their lifespan, to uphold the rights of the people, fulfil the duties of their faith, gain in [spiritual] honor, earn greater merit, perform a virtuous deed, or acquire knowledge, they will deeply regret having ever lived such a day.

Of course, you should set aside time for your family and your schooling or job; but under no circumstances should you let your worldly schedule prevent you from establishing the ritual prayer in congregation as much as you can. If there is not a mosque close by, you should gather those around you in your workplace or school and have one person act as the caller to prayer (*mu'adhdhin*) and another the imam to lead the worship.

What should we start and end our day with? How can we effectively shift from our worldly mode to a worship mode?

1 . The Prophet's Night Vigil (al-Witr an-Nabawī)[8]

The believer should begin their day by waking up one hour before the dawn prayer (or, at the very least, a little before the dawn prayer) to perform five sets of two-cycle prayers capped by a one-cycle prayer. In this worship, the believer should manifest humility and helplessness before the Lord, for the prayer is supposed to represent total devotion to Him. This is particularly applicable for the night vigil which is the best ritual worship after the five prescribed prayers, as attested to by at least one *ḥadīth*[9] of the Prophet (God bless him and grant him peace).

Between each prayer unit, the worshipper should beseech their Lord with tears flowing down their face. They should see from themselves nothing but negligence, deficiency, helplessness, and need; they should see whatever virtues they possess as being nothing more than a gift from the Maker, praising Him for such generosity.

---

[8] TN: The Prophet's night vigil (*al-witr an-nabawī*) is made up of five sets of two-unit prayers [one unit = *rakʿah*, literally "bowing"], the last of which is called *rakʿatā ash-shafʿ*, followed by a one-unit prayer called *rakʿat al-witr*.

[9] TN: A report about the Prophet (God bless him and grant him peace).

"Truly, those who succeed are those who purify it [the soul] (91:9): The key to perfecting the soul lies in precisely recognizing its imperfection, the key to its power lies in acknowledging its very powerlessness before Him (glorified is He), while its affluence lies in seeing nothing but its poverty and dire need.

Imām Aḥmad has narrated on the authority of al-Muṭṭalib that the Prophet (God bless him and grant him peace) instructed:

> *In the night vigil, you should end each prayer set with a recitation of the tashahhud*[10]*, then stretching out your hands to form a mask, bearing your wretchedness and helplessness, and imploring: "O Lord! O Lord!" - for to fail to do this results in an imperfect prayer (literally: a prematurely-born baby). Shuʿba then inquired: "Their prayer will be imperfect?" "Indeed." "What does it mean to stretch out your hands to form a mask?" - the Prophet demonstrated by covering his face with his hands.*

---

[10] TN: A ritual invocation consisting of saluting God, uttering the two Testimonies of Faith (*ash-shahādatān*), and asking God to shed His peace and blessings upon the Prophet.

In his *Ṣaḥīḥ*[11], Ibn Ḥibbān reports the following statement of the Messenger (God bless him and grant him peace) on the authority of Ibn Masʿūd (God be pleased with him):

Our Lord is amazed at two types of people. One leaves their spouse and bed [in the middle of the night] to establish the night vigil. The Lord (exalted is He) proclaims to His angels: "Look at My servant who has risen from sleep and left their beloved spouse to seek My favor and out of trembling fear for My wrath!..."

Upon finishing the night vigil, the believer should sit down and pray to the Lord for forgiveness. As Sūrat adh-Dhārīyāt (51:17-18) describes those who will achieve the everlasting bliss of Paradise:

> *They were in the habit of sleeping but little by night, and in the hours of early dawn, praying (to God) for forgiveness.*

[11] TN: Book compiling authenticated reports about the Prophet.

2 . A Reward Equal to the Greater Pilgrimage (Ḥajj) and the Lesser Pilgrimage (ʿUmra)

The time from after the dawn prayer until sunrise is a blessed one which the believer should spend reciting and memorizing Qurʾān and engaging in remembrance of God (*dhikr*), for this is a custom of the Prophet. Imām Aḥmad and the other authors of the *Sunan* (books of authenticated *ḥadīths*) have reported from the Messenger (God bless him and grant him peace):

> *O Lord, shed your blessings on those activities of my community (umma) performed in the early morning.*

In this vein, Tirmidhī has related this Prophetic counsel:

> *Establishing the dawn prayer in congregation, sitting down to engage in remembrance of God until sunrise, and finishing this session off with a two-cycle prayer set merits the same reward as performing the Greater Pilgrimage or the Lesser Pilgrimage. (The Messenger [God bless him and grant him peace] then reiterated thrice: "[A] full and complete [pilgrimage], full and complete,*

> *full and complete.") [Recorded by Tirmidhī who graded the ḥadīth's chain as fairly strong, but lacking in corroboration (ḥasan gharīb).]*

3 . The Prayer of Those Who Constantly Turn to Their Lord (al-Awwābūn)

Ṣalāt aḍ-Ḍuḥā, which consists of performing one to four two-cycle prayers in the late morning, is the custom of those who constantly turn to God (*al-awwābūn*). As the Messenger (God bless him and grant him peace) has related from his Lord:

> *O child of Adam, perform for My sake two two-cycle prayers in the beginning of the daytime and I shall take care of you until the end of that day.*

4 . A House in Paradise

It is a well-established custom of the Prophet to perform the following prayers in addition to the five mandatory ones:

- one two-cycle prayer anytime after performing the ablution (*al-wuḍū'*) - which was the custom of the noble Bilāl;

- one two-cycle prayer before the dawn prayer;
- two two-cycle prayers before the noon prayer (which open the gates of Heaven) and one after;
- one two-cycle prayer before the afternoon prayer;
- one two-cycle prayer before the sunset prayer and three after;
- and one two-cycle prayer before and two after the evening prayer.

Each day, a house is built in Paradise for those who make this their practice, as Imām Muslim (*inter alia*) has relayed from the Messenger (God bless him and grant him peace). If you cannot wake up before the dawn prayer, then perform the night vigil (*ṣalāt al-witr*) before going to sleep, although it is superior to perform it immediately before dawn.

5. The Lucrative Trade

Reading a litany (*wird*) from the Qurʾān with presence, humility, and contemplation once in the morning and once in the evening is a lucrative trade that will help you prosper forever. As Imām Muslim has relayed from the Messenger (God bless him and grant him peace):

Recite the Qurʾān, for it will act as an intercessor on the Day of Judgement for those who recited it.

Reading at least two sections (*ḥizb*) of the Qurʾān per day has been counseled by the Prophet so that one may complete the whole Qurʾān within thirty days. Conversely, to leave aside the Book and fail to celebrate the Message of the Divine is to neglect one's faith.

The more pure the soul, the more one will benefit from such a reading; as ʿUthmān b. ʿAffān (God be pleased with him) once remarked: "Had your hearts been truly pure, you would never have had enough of reciting the Book of your Lord."

O Lord, let the Holy Qurʾān be the joy of our hearts and the dispeller of our worries!

6 . Meritorious Sections of the Qurʾān

There are several reports from the Prophet on the merits of reciting certain passages of the Book, which can serve to safeguard us from evil, dispel our worries, wipe out our sins, or raise us to a more elevated station. It is from such passages of the Qurʾān that the believer should constitute their daily litany, listed below.

First, you should recite the *isti'ādha* formula (*a'ūdhu bi-Llāhi min ash-Shayṭān ar-Rajīm* ["I seek refuge with God from the Evil One"]) and the basmala (*bismi Llāhi ar-Raḥmāni ar-Raḥīm* ["In the Name of God, the Most Gracious, the Most Merciful"]). Then, recite the following from the Qur'ān (numbering based on the Ḥafṣ version):

Chapter 1 ♦ 2:1-5 ♦ 2:255-57 ♦ 2:284-86 ♦ 3:1-9, 18, 19, 26, 27, 190-200 ♦ 9:128-29 (seven times) ♦ 18:107-10 ♦ Chapter 32 ♦ Chapter 36 ♦ 40:1-3 ♦ Chapter 44 ♦ 48:29 ♦ Chapter 56.

Then recite al-Musabbiḥāt (the chapters that begin with the formulaic glorification of God): 57, 59, 61, 62, and 64.

Then recite the ending chapters of the Qur'ān: 67, 87, 93, 94, 96, 97, 99 (four times); 102, 103 (twice); 106, 107, 108 (three times); 109 (four times); 110 (four times); 112 (three times); 113 and 114.

Then end with the first chapter (al-Fātiḥa) and 2:1-5.

7. The Renewal of Faith

You should set aside three sessions (fifteen minutes each) to focus on chanting the Blessed Statement (*al-Kalima aṭ-Ṭayyiba*), "There is no god but God" (*lā ilāha illallāh*), which represents the highest branch of faith. By chanting this formula with presence of mind, your faith will be renewed, as Imām Aḥmad has narrated in the following *ḥadīth* from the Messenger (God bless him and grant him peace) with a fairly-strong (*ḥasan*) chain of transmission:

> "Make sure to renew your faith."
>
> "Messenger of God - and how should we do that?"
>
> "Say: 'There is no god but God (*lā ilāha illallāh*)' as often as you can."

Hence, you must make it a habit to have this on your lips constantly: "Engage in remembrance of God until they accuse you of insanity." [Ibn Ḥibbān and al-Ḥākim, the latter grading the *ḥadīth* authentic (*ṣaḥīḥ*).]

8 . Becoming Close to the Messenger (God Bless Him and Grant Him Peace)

You should chant blessings and salutations on the Prophet at least three hundred times a day, and particularly on the night of Thursday and the day of Friday. By this does the Lord redeem us from the depths of darkness into the light: "Those who will most be deserving of my company on the Day of Resurrection will be those who had most often asked God to shed His blessings on me." [Tirmidhī and Ibn Ḥibbān on the authority of Ibn Masʿūd.]

Abū Dāwūd and an-Nasāʾī have also related on the authority of Abū Hurayra (God be pleased with him) the following from the Prophet (God bless him and grant him peace):

> *Whoever aspires to the Greatest Reward should recite: "O Lord, shed Your blessings upon Muḥammad the Prophet, his wives, his descendants, and his family, just as You have shed your blessings upon the Household of Abraham, for You are worthy of all praise, worthy of all glory.*

9. The Etiquette of Sleep

Before going to sleep, turn yourself toward God (exalted be He) and call yourself to account for how you spent your day for, as Maymūn b. Mahrān, a noble *tābiʿī* from the generation after the Companions, said, "The true believer calls themselves to account more stringently than the tyrant ruler calls their subjects to account, or more stringently than the miserly businessman calls their partners to account." So before sleep, renew your repentance to the Lord; foster a state of ritual purity (*ṭahāra*) and engage in the Divine remembrance (*dhikr*) with the best of intentions. Let the last moments of your wakefulness be moments wherein you pray to the Lord to open to you the many paths of *jihād* and the reaching of His Presence. For whoever has not made the intention to strive for the sake of God, will die as a pagan, as the beloved Messenger (God bless him and grant him peace) declared. Accordingly, do not stay up late needlessly, for those whose tomorrow is not better than their yesterday are losers.

10 . The Duties of the Student of Knowledge

If you are a seeker of knowledge, make the time to properly attend to your studies. After establishing the ritual prayer, reciting the Qur'ān, and engaging in the Divine remembrance, your number-one priority is to acquire the basic teachings of the faith. After that, your priority is to succeed in your academic studies, for academic studying is the *jihād* of this stage of your life. Accordingly, focus on those books that will benefit you both in this world and in the Hereafter. As a sage once remarked, Tell me what books you read, and I can tell you who you are.

11 . Sessions of Faith, Trips for Seeking Knowledge, and Missions for Calling Others to the Faith

Devote at least one hour for a session of faith with your brethren so that you may be of those who rejoice in the Gardens of Paradise, as the beloved Messenger (God bless him and grant him peace) informed us. Also, devote time to trips for seeking knowledge and missions to call others to the faith, for to have God guide one person through you is better than all that upon which the sun rises.

12 . No Action without Knowledge

Devote a small amount of your day to studying user-friendly books which instruct the layman in how to master ritual purity and ritual prayer, in addition to the other major acts of worship. For God (exalted is He) does not accept sincere acts unless they are also ritually correct, that is, in conformity with the Prophet's Tradition.

13 . The Value of Time

As al-Ḥasan al-Baṣrī (God have mercy upon him) once said, "Child of Adam, you are nothing but a number of days: with the passing of each day, a part of you is gone." Therefore, budget your time like money: be miserly and avoid wasting it in heedless trivialities. Always keep in mind that the time you will in hindsight realize had been wasted - when it will be too late for this regret to make any difference - will be that time in which you failed to remember the Lord (exalted is He) with your tongue and your heart and when you failed to serve His Cause. Similarly, you should not waste others' time by coming late to your meetings with them or by socializing for hours on end.

14 . The Supplication of Spiritual Bond (Duʿāʾ ar-Rābiṭa)[12]

• *Supplication in Islam*

Supplication (*duʿāʾ*) is the very essence of worship. There are two types of supplication: those prayers meant to express your specific needs, and those meant to manifest your devotion. Indeed, all acts of worship can be categorized as supplication of the second type. If the only merit of invocation were that it brought you closer to the Lord (glorified be He), that would be enough, but the Messenger (God bless him and grant him peace) further taught us that, "There is nothing that God holds in more esteem than His servant's invocation." [Tirmidhī, Aḥmad, Ibn Mājah]

• *The Supplication of the Throne-Bearers for the Believers*

Since man is incapable of discerning his true interests, the Lord (exalted is He) has given him invocations to say from the Qurʾān and the Prophetic Tradition. Among the supplications noted by the Qurʾān are those of the angels (peace

[12] The name of an invocation that connects us to our brethren in the faith, from both past and future generations.

be upon them) for the righteous believers; and this passage indirectly encourages us to pray for our brethren:

> *Those who sustain the Throne (of God) and those around it sing the glory and praises of their Lord, affirm their belief in Him, and implore Him for the forgiveness of those who believe: 'Our Lord! You encompass all things in Your mercy and knowledge, so forgive those who turn in repentance to You and follow Your path, and preserve them from the Blazing Fire! Grant to them, O Lord, that they enter the Gardens of Eternity which You have promised to them, and to the righteous among their parents, spouses, and children. For You are the Exalted in Might, the One Full of Wisdom. And preserve them also from all evil deeds; anyone whom You preserve from evil deeds on that Day You will truly have shown great mercy. And that is the highest achievement.* [40:7-9]

• ***With What Words Should We Pray? To Whom Should We Direct Our Prayers?***

Among the signs of God's mercy is that He has taught His servants not only how to ritually worship Him but also how to supplicate Him. The best of supplications are those which He Himself has formulated for us, for they are His words from Him to Him.

Among the teachings of the Holy Qur'ān on this issue are that we pray for those who embraced the faith before us (such as our father Adam and our mother Eve [God grant them peace]) as well as our predecessors from whom the faith has been passed down, since it is from them that we have been able to learn Islam. Our forbearers were faithful in their passing down of this tradition, possessed of integrity in their practical work, paragons of sincerity for God's cause.

"Our Lord! Forgive us and our brethren who before us entered into the faith, and leave not in our hearts any rancor against those who have believed. Our Lord! You are indeed Full of Kindness, Most Merciful." [59:10]

• *The Supplication of Spiritual Bond to Unite Companionship with Community*

What Imām al-Bannā (God have mercy on him) named the Litany of Spiritual Bond (*wird ar-rābiṭa*) is an expression of the pact of brotherhood among the believers. We should emphasize the utter necessity of reciting the Supplication of Spiritual Bond (*duʿāʾ ar-rābiṭa*) for bringing the *Umma* together. By constantly meeting with each other, standing together in prayer, working together, and praying the Supplication of Spiritual Bond, the believers foster the virtue of companionship and community (*aṣ-ṣuḥba wa-l-jamāʿa*)[13] so that the communion of believers is not just a body, but a body with a soul, so that their companionship is not just the friendship between two isolated individuals, but the brotherhood of a community.

• *The Fruit of the Supplication of Spiritual Bond*

By articulating this ritual invocation, the believer comes to see themselves as part of the Radiant Procession of faith and

[13] TN: Companionship and Community (*aṣ-ṣuḥba wa-l-jamāʿa*), the first of the Ten Virtues espoused by Imām Abdessalam Yassine, entails tutelage under a guide who, unlike in the traditional Sufi orders, guides you in not only spiritual but also in temporal matters, and hence directs you to all the different paths of *jihād*: first and foremost, the inward *jihād* of the self (hence the need for community) as well as that *jihād* which is not merely military but which entails helping the *Umma* acquire all the means (scientific, industrial, technological) which will enable it to manifest its message of mercy to mankind. In other words, the believer cannot attain true spiritual excellence without participating in a communitarian project just as the Companions themselves had (God be pleased with them).

jihād that stretches across time from Adam (peace be upon him) to the Day of Resurrection and as part of the Blessed Community under the protection of the Lord (exalted be He). Their spiritual link to their other brethren grows stronger and stronger, even if they are physically separated from each other. The centrality of this prayer is further underlined by the fact that it is an integral part of the *tashahhud*: "Peace be upon us and upon all God's righteous servants"; the Prophet (God bless him and grant him peace) expounded that "Whenever [the Muslim in prayer] pronounces this invocation, it reaches all of God's righteous servants in heaven and on earth." [Muslim]

• *Invoking the Divine for the Sake of Your Brethren is a Sign of Lofty Character*

The Companions (God be pleased with them) followed the Glorious Qur'ān and the Noble Tradition of the Prophet, praying for each other in the middle of the night to affirm that their hearts were not only free of rancor, but indeed full of love for their fellow believers. In his *Shuʿab al-Īmān* (Branches of Faith), *al-Bayhaqī* reports from Umm ad-Dardā':

Abū ad-Dardāʾ once held a night vigil, in which he kept shedding tears and crying, 'O Lord! Refine my character just as You originally created me in the best of fashions!' This he did until the break of dawn. I [Umm ad-Dardāʾ] asked him, 'Why did you keep repeating a prayer about character?' 'Umm ad-Dardāʾ: If the Muslim servant keeps refining their character, they may be admitted to Paradise. Conversely, if they keep letting their character degrade, they will enter Hell. Not to mention that it is possible for the Muslim servant to have their sins forgiven while they are sound asleep.' 'How is that possible??' 'If their brother or sister stays up at night and prays to God (exalted be He) for them, then God may forgive that person as well as the person who prayed for them.'

- ***Prayers for the Believer in Their Absence are Answered***

Whenever one Companion would meet another, the first would ask the second to pray for them - particularly if the latter were about to travel to that holy of holies, Mecca. Muslim and Abū Dāwūd have related an anecdote from ʿAbdullāh b. Safwān b. Umayya b. Khalaf (the son-in-law of the aforementioned Abū ad-Dardā'):

> *Once, when I traveled to Syria, I visited Abū ad-Dardā''s house. He was not home but his wife, Umm ad-Dardā', was, and she asked me, 'Do you intend to perform the pilgrimage this year?' 'Yes.' 'Then pray for me, since the Messenger (God bless him and grant him peace) used to say, "When a Muslim prays for their brother or sister in their absence, their prayers are answered. And ever-present is an angel who pronounces for such a person, 'Amen! And your reward shall be the same.'"' I then went out and came across Abū ad-Dardā' in the market. He too related the same ḥadīth to me.*

Once, when 'Umar b. al-Khaṭṭāb (God be pleased with him) asked the Messenger (God bless him and grant him peace) permission to perform the lesser pilgrimage (*'umra*), the Prophet replied: "Brother, do not forget to include me in your prayers." [Tirmidhī, Ibn Mājah, Abū Dāwūd. The version given here is that of Tirmidhī, who authenticated the report.]

Ibn Ḥibbān in his Ṣaḥīḥ, and al-Bazzār in his Musnad have reported from Lady 'Ā'isha (God be pleased with her):

Once, when I saw that the Messenger (God bless him and grant him peace) was in a good mood, I said, 'Messenger of God, pray to God for me!' 'O Lord, forgive 'Ā'isha all her sins, past and future, inward and outward.' This prompted 'Ā'isha to laugh until her head fell into her lap. 'Has my supplication pleased you?' 'How could it not??' The Prophet (God bless him and grant him peace) then said: 'That is the supplication that I say in every ritual prayer for my Umma.'

- ***What is the Foundation of Supplication?***

Our prayers will not be answered until they are substantiated by righteous deeds, as evidenced by Sūrat Āl 'Imrān, āya 195:

And their Lord responded to them, "Never will I allow to be lost the work of [any] worker among you, whether male or female; you are of one another. So those who emigrated or were evicted from their homes or were harmed in My cause or fought or were killed - I will surely remove from them their misdeeds, and I will surely admit them

> *to gardens beneath which rivers flow as reward from God, and God has with Him the best reward. [3:195]*

The first chapter of the Qur'ān, Sūrat al-Fātiḥa, emphasizes that the "right Way" prayed for by the believers (1:6) is the Way of the previous generations of believers - the prophets, the sincere, the martyrs, and the righteous on whom the Lord bestowed His grace. And what better company could you be included with? Therefore, by observing the Day and Night Schedule of the Believer and by cultivating the ties of kinship, the believer takes on the Way of those possessed of the Divine grace. And thus does the Supplication of Spiritual Bond bring the believer one more step toward spiritual wakefulness - but again, this prayer only has any force if it is combined with love in God, good manners, and righteous deeds.

• *Some Points of Etiquette for Supplication*

Supplicating the Divine has its own procedures of etiquette. Ibn ʿAṭāʾ Illāh as-Sakandarī said:

> *Supplication has its pillars, wings, means, and appointed time. With its pillars, it becomes firm; with its wings, it flies into the heavens; with its*

prescribed time, it is granted success; and with its means, it becomes effective. The pillars refer to mindfulness, compassion, humility, and reverence. The wings are integrity. The prescribed time is the early hours before dawn. And the means are praying to God to shed His benedictions upon Muḥammad (God bless him and grant him peace).

- ***"...And to Our Brethren Who Embraced Faith before Us"***

The believer should perform the Supplication of Spiritual Bond in the early hours before dawn when the Lord (exalted be He) descends to the First Heaven to ask after those seeking repentance, although the believer can express this prayer at any time. The worshipper should open their prayer by reciting the first chapter of the Qurʾān and then sending benedictions upon the Prophet (God bless him and grant him peace). Then, the supplicant should ask God to forgive their own sins and to grant to them and to their parents, spouse, children, and other relatives all the good things of this world and the Hereafter. Then they should ask God to shower His grace and peace upon all of His prophets, from Adam to Muḥammad, naming aloud those prophets individually mentioned in the Qur'ān, keeping in mind the saying of the Master of Messengers: "Whenever you salute me, salute also the other Messengers, for I am but one of them."

Similarly, ath-Tha'labī has reported from Abū Sa'īd al-Khudrī that the Messenger (God bless him and grant him peace) would sometimes say at the end of his ritual prayer, or alternatively before taking leave of his Companions:

> *Glory be to your Lord, the Lord of honor and power, Who is free from all that they ascribe to Him! Peace be upon the Messengers, and praise be to God, the Lord and Cherisher of the Universe. [182-37:180]*

Ibn Abī Hāthim has narrated on the authority of ash-Sha'bī and al-Baghawī, who in turn have reported on the authority of 'Alī (may God honor him) from the Messenger (God bless him and grant him peace):

> *Whoever seeks the Fullest Measure (al-mikyāl al-awfā) on the Day of Resurrection should recite, before taking leave of any sort of gathering: 'Glory be to your Lord, the Lord of honor and power, Who is free from all that they ascribe to Him! Peace be*

upon the Messengers, and praise be to God, the Lord and Cherisher of the Universe.'

Note that the phrase *al-mikyāl al-awfā* is also used in reference to the reward of praying upon the Prophet.

Then the worshipper should ask the Lord to bestow His felicitous salutations and His contentment upon the Prophet's family, descendants, and spouses, mentioning as many by name as possible. Then the worshipper should beseech God to bestow His contentment on the Rightly-Guided Caliphs, the Ten Companions promised Paradise[14], and then the other Companions, again by name if possible. Then the worshipper should pray for the Lord's mercy upon the second generation of Muslims (*at-tābiʿūn*) and upon the scholars and righteous men and women of this Umma, by name for those whose name they know.

Then comes the Qurʾānic invocation: "Our Lord! Forgive us as well as our brethren who came before us in faith, and put not in our hearts any resentment against those who have

---

[14] TN: The ten Companions whom the Prophet (God bless him and grant him peace) promised Paradise: the four Rightly-Guided Caliphs (Abū Bakr, ʿUmar, ʿUthmān, ʿAlī), Ṭalḥa b. ʿUbaydillāh, az-Zubayr b. al-ʿAwāmm, Saʿd b. Abī Waqqāṣ, Saʿīd b. Zayd, Abū ʿUbayda b. al-Jarrāḥ, and ʿAbd ar-Raḥmān b. ʿAwf.

believed. Our Lord, You are indeed Full of Kindness, Most Merciful." [59:10]

Then the supplicant lays before God all the *Umma's* woes and asks Him for forgiveness and for victory for all those fighting and striving in His cause.

Then they mention by name all those with whom they share a tie of love and struggle.

Then they ask mercy, forgiveness, and all the good things of this world and the Hereafter for the *Umma of Muḥammad*, and that they be united under a true *khilāfa* and granted victory over their enemies. Lastly, the believer seals the invocation with benedictions upon the Messenger.

• *Supplication as an Act of Remembrance of the Hereafter*

How transcendent is that heart that, in those moments of intimate invocation, turns entirely toward God! How present the remembrance of the Hereafter through the daily salutation of those pure souls! Indeed, God loves best the servant's abstaining from worldly concerns by immersing themselves in such remembrance. On top of which, "The acts that God loves best are those that one performs regularly." [Bukhārī]

• *Supplication & Dedication of Worship for the Sake of Others*

After reciting the Prayer of Spiritual Bond, the worshipper should recite passages of the Qurʾān with the intention of dedicating their reward to all pure souls, with some passages set aside particularly for one's parents. Al-Ḥāfiẓ ʿAbdullāh b. aṣ-Ṣiddīq al-Ghumārī (God have mercy upon him) has penned a valuable booklet on this subject: *Authentic Texts Demonstrating that the Reward of Reciting the Qurʾān for Others Reaches Their Souls* (Tawḍīḥ al-Bayān fī Wuṣūl Thawāb al-Qurʾān).

• *Presence & Humility*

An important feature of the Prophetic Tradition is that it provides us with multiple prayers for a single occasion, thus giving us a variety of supplications to choose from, thereby helping us to avoid mindlessly reciting these prayers in a rote fashion. As Tirmidhī and al-Ḥākim have reported from the Messenger (God bless him and grant him peace): "Know that God does not answer any prayer emanating from a heedless heart." Hence, the believer should avoid praying the Prayer of Spiritual Bond with a set formula, but should pray it with words that spring forth spontaneously from a sense of humility and reverence.

Dear brothers and sisters:

In the end, we ask the Divine, the Most Kind and Most Merciful, to guide us to good, to make us ever-aware of our powerlessness before Him, and to make us His instruments in restoring the *Umma* to its glory.

And our ending prayer is: Praise be to God, the Lord and Sustainer of the universe, and grace and peace upon the Messenger Muḥammad, his family, Companions, brethren, and party.

By the Same Author

- ***Translated into English:***

1. Memorandum: To Him Who Is Concerned (An open letter to the new King of Morocco), 1999.

2. Winning the Modern World for Islam, 2000.

3. The Muslim Mind on Trial: Divine Revelation versus Secular Rationalism, 2003.

4. Day and Night Schedule of the Believer (A book in Arabic and English), 2007.

5. The Last Testament, 2014.

6. The Muslim Woman: Journey into the Light - Volume 1, 2016.

- ***In Arabic:***

1. Islam between the Appeal and the State, 1972.
2. Tomorrow Islam, 1973.
3. Islam - or the Flood (An Open Letter to the late King of Morocco), 1974.
4. The Royal Centennial Missive in the Balance of Islam, 1980.
5. The Prophetic Method [al-Minhāj an-Nabawi], 1982.
6. Islam and the Challenge of Marxism-Leninism, 1987.
7. Exemplary Men (1st in the series Al-Ihssān), 1988.
8. Introductions to the Method, 1989.
9. Islam and the Challenge of Secular Nationalism, 1989.
10. Reflections on Islamic Jurisprudence and History, 1989.
11. Spiritual Gems (A Collection of Poems), 1992.
12. The Muslim Mind on Trial: Divine Revelation versus Secular Rationalism, 1994.

13. A Dialogue with Honorable Democrats, 1994.
14. Letter of Reminder (1st in the series Rasa'il Al-Ihsān), 1995.
15. On the Economy, 1995.
16. Letter to Students and to all Muslims (2nd in the series Rassa'il Al-Ihssân), 1995.
17. Guide to Believing Women, 1996.
18. Shūra and Democracy, 1996.
19. Poetic Exhortations (3rd in the series Rasa'il Al-Ihsān), 1996.
20. Dialogue of the Past and the Future, 1997.
21. Dialogue with an Amazighit Friend, 1997.
22. Spirituality [Al-Ihssān] V1, 1998.
23. How Shall We Renew Our Faith, How Do We Advise for God's Sake and His Messenger? (1st in the series "The Prophetic Method Discourses"), 1998.
24. Al-Fitra and Curing the Hearts, 1998 (2nd in the series "The Prophetic Method Discourses"), 1998.

25. Spirituality [Al-Ihssān] V2, 1999.
26. Sound Hearts (3rd in the series “The Prophetic Method Discourses”), 1999.
27. Braving the Obstacles (4th in the series “The Prophetic Method Discourses”), 1999.
28. Justice: Islamists and Power, 2000.
29. Bunches of Grapes (A Collection of Poems in 7 volumes), 2000-2017.
30. The Scholarly Treatise, 2001.
31. Caliphate and Monarchy, 2001.
32. Exemplary Men of Uprising and Reform, 2001.
33. Day and Night Schedule of the Believer, 2002.
34. The Price (5th in the series “The Prophetic Method Discourses”), 2004.
35. God’s Custom, 2005.
36. Introductions to the Future of Islam, 2005.
37. Day and Night Schedule of the Believer, 2007.

38. Leadership of the Umma, 2009.
39. Qur'ān and Prophecy, 2010.
40. Bonding the Muslim Community, 2011.
41. Branches of Faith (in 2 volumes), 2017.

- ***Translated into Arabic:***

    1. Toward a Dialogue with our Westernized Elite, 1980
    2. Memorandum: To Whom It May Concern, 1999
    3. Winning the Modern World for Islam, 2000

- ***In French:***

1. The Islamic Method of Revolution, 1980.
2. Toward a Dialogue with our Westernized Elite, 1980.
3. Winning the Modern World for Islam, 1998.
4. Memorandum: To Him Who Is Concerned (An open letter to the new King of Morocco), 1999.

- ***Translated into French:***

1. The Last Testament, 2014.
2. Reflections on Islamic Jurisprudence and History, 2015.

- ***Translated into German:***

    1. Memorandum: To Him Who Is Concerned (An open letter to the new King of Morocco), 1999.

    2. Winning the Modern World for Islam (Translation), 2000.

    3. Day and Night Schedule of the Believer (Translation), 2013.

- ***Translated into Turkish:***

    1. The Prophetic Method [al-Minhāj an-Nabawi], 2012.
    2. God's Custom, 2012.
    3. Caliphate and Monarchy, 2012.
    4. Exemplary Men of Uprising and Reform, 2012.
    5. The Last Testament, 2013.

- ***Translated into Italian:***

    1. Day and Night Schedule of the Believer, 2013.
    2. The Last Testament, 2014.
    3. Winning the Modern World for Islam, 2015.

4. Exemplary Men (1st in the series Al-Ihssān), 2016.

- ***Translated into Spanish:***

1. Memorandum: To Him Who Is Concerned (An open letter to the new King of Morocco), 1999.
2. The Last Testament, 2014.

- ***Translated into Urdu:***

1. Winning the Modern World for Islam, 2017.

- ***Translated into Russian:***

1. The Muslim Mind on Trial: Divine Revelation versus Secular Rationalism, 2014.

- ***Translated into Ukrainian:***

1. The Muslim Mind on Trial: Divine Revelation versus Secular Rationalism, 2014.

Note

Note

Note

JSP

Justice & Spirituality
Publishing